I0060037

Foreword by Peggy McColl, New York T...

50 Simple Ways to Increase Brand Visibility

Jae M. Rang, MAS

Author of "SENSORY MEDIA, Discover the Way to Anchor Your Brand and Be Memorable"

What people are saying about

50 Simple Ways to Increase Brand Visibility

"Jae AGAIN delivers fabulous insights and practical applications to keep our brand, front and centre, both personally and professionally".

~ *Michele Bailey, CEO & Founder: Blazing Designs, Ontario, Canada*

"This book has something for every size of business. We've already taken action on ideas shared in Jae's book, *50 Simple Ways to Increase Brand Visibility*. This book is packed full of great investment ideas that range from "*it costs NOTHING*" to "*it costs a little MORE*". We will continue to review this book frequently to implement more ideas that will keep our brand forefront in the market".

~ *Linda McLean, #1 International Best Selling Author,*
CEO & Founder of McLean International LLC., Nevada, U.S.A.

"Highly informative and at times humorous, Jae M Rang wowed me with her fifty ways to win at engaging with existing and potential customers alike. So many great ideas!".

~ *Eugenie D. Basu, MBA, Coach, Speaker, Texas, U.S.A.*

"I found myself reading line-after-line with a few 'aha' moments along the way... Reading 50 ways to increase brand awareness and imagining how I can incorporate these ideas into my business seem so simple, yet were off my radar. Looks like we will be busy rejuvenating our brand and having fun doing it!"

~ *Debbie Gust, President, WOW Factor Desserts, Alberta, Canada*

"Jae Rang shares her insights and wealth of experience with SENSORY MEDIA and how it supports branding in her book, *50 Simple Ways to Increase Brand Visibility*. The book offers a great selection of fresh and modern ways to increase the visibility of any brand. "50 Simple Ways…" is a must-read for a better understanding the impact promotional products can have on your brand when the human element is taken into consideration."

~ *Elizabeth Hueston, Director of Marketing, Guest Supply Canada, Ontario, Canada*

"If an apple-a-day keeps the doctor away then Jae M. Rang's innovative book, *50 Simple Ways to Increase Brand Visibility*, is the right "cure all" for brand stagnation. Implementing any one of Jae's ideas can provide a decent ROI for the time you devote to it. Implementing all 50… Priceless!"

~ *Lennox Cornwall, Author, entrepreneur & inventor, Trinidad and Tobago*

"Although Jae has just shared a whopping FIFTY easily implementable ideas, I know from personal experience working with her that she has endless creative approaches to helping your brand shine. Join her mailing list and find out for yourself. Her enthusiasm for crafting the perfect customer experience may even rub off on you."

~ *Kaz Lefave, author of "Nemecene: The Epoch of Redress", Ontario, Canada*

*This book is dedicated to
my many, many, many teachers*

50 Simple Ways to Increase Brand Visibility

By Jae M. Rang, MAS

Published by Hasmark Publishing

Copyright© 2016 Jae M Rang

First Edition, 2016

No part of this book may be reproduced or transmitted in any form or by any means, electronic or mechanical, including photocopying, recording or by any information storage and retrieval system, without written permission from the author, except for the inclusion of brief quotations in a review.

Limit of Liability and Disclaimer of Warranty: The publisher has used its best efforts in preparing this book, and the information provided herein is provided "as is."

The publisher does not have control over and does not assume responsibility for the author or third party websites. Neither the publisher nor the individual author(s) shall be liable for any physical, psychological, emotional, financial, or commercial damages, including, but not limited to, special, incidental, consequential, or other damages.

Permission should be addressed to: Jae M Rang, MAS and email to 50simplyways@jaeassociates.com

Cover Design:
Patti Knoles
www.VirtualGraphicArtsDepartment.com

Layout:
Hasmark Publishing, Anne Karklins

ISBN: 978-1-988071-18-3
ISBN: 1-988071-18-6

Acknowledgements

One of the many things I have learned from my friend, Bob Proctor (Author: *You Were Born Rich*) is that everything starts with a decision. The decision to write this book came out of nowhere – like a lightening bolt – and with the inspiration to offer insights that I've used for decades. The urge to capture the information was so powerful that I wrote the book in under 48 hours.

My inspiration came from a conversation with Peggy McColl. We spent a few hours together at her home recently, discussing things we both were working on and the potential synergy. I was so inspired by her energy, enthusiasm, willingness to give, and success that I jumped on this idea to share my insights. I am very thankful for her mentorship and the thoughtful foreword she wrote.

My go-to person when I have any idea is my son, William. He has such a great mind and a big heart. Amidst a jammed university schedule, he happily carved out brainstorming time to help me get started. I am so grateful for him always and in so many ways.

My close colleague, Gabriella Morfesis, is my biggest cheerleader at work. Gabriella always says the reason we do so well is because we care. She's right. We do. She also generously entertains the many, many times I think out loud, adding ways in which we can be even better.

This is the second cover Patti Knoles has done for me that has been right on point. Then again, it's no surprise as Patti is the designer of choice to many best-selling authors around the world. What a pro.

Big thanks to my Elite Inner Circle partners, Women Presidents' Organization sisters, and Proctor Gallagher Institute fellow Experts Michele Bailey, Linda McLean, Eugenie Basu, Debbie Gust, Lennox Cornwall, Kaz LeFave and Elizabeth Hueston, who were kind enough to fit doing a review into their already demanding schedules. And to Amy Stoehr for her insightful use of her red pen. I am so grateful for the love and energy we all share.

A world of appreciation goes to Gina Hayden, Bob Proctor, Kathy Perry, Robin Cawkell, Virginia Clutsam, Sandy Gallagher, Dean Parris, Danilee Trott, Evelyn Barnett, Tatiana Read, Peggy Grall, Rasheeda Burgess, Cynthia Kersey, Thomas Dunstan, Tara Curtis, Laura Williams, Kaz LeFave, Marty Britton, Cory Kelly, Peggy McColl, Michele Bailey, Elizabeth Hueston, Brian Proctor, and Ann Elliott for their confidence in us, and for being open to creative opportunities to build together. It's a distinct pleasure working with these exceptional individuals and their teams.

Foreword

The fact that you are holding this book in your hands is already separating you from the rest. Good for you! And, that is precisely what it will bring... good for you and good for your business!

We live in a wonderful world of opportunity. The opportunity to choose, the opportunity to grow, the opportunity to expand and the opportunity to have a successful business and truly live a dream-life doing work that is deeply meaningful. But, doing work that is meaningful and living your life on purpose is not enough, we must take steps toward standing out from the rest.

If you are in business today you probably already know you must be focused on building and expanding your brand. You must find ways to stand out from the rest; get noticed and invite clients to make a decision to choose you, your products and/or service and your brand.

My friend, Jae M. Rang, is a successful entrepreneur who has built a very successful business. The depth of her knowledge, inquisitive nature and desire to help others reach their potential is second to none. Jae is always looking for the reason why things are as they are, then finding ways to do them better. She never stops thinking and as a result, continues to produce great results.

Jae's first book, *SENSORY MEDIA: Discover the Way to Anchor Your Brand and Be Memorable* had even her industry professionals applauding. Jae recognized, through her study of the mind, the value of this tangible medium in making brand experiences memorable. But Jae also recognizes that a brand is way more than a logo or the product it's printed on. A brand starts with people.

In "50 Simple Ways to Improve Brand Visibility", Jae has cleverly integrated some really innovative ways to create brand visibility both on-line and off-line. Whether you use one, two or all fifty of Jae's recommendations, you will very likely experience a positive result. I am grateful Jae took the time to put together this valuable resource and I believe you will be too.

Dig in, devour, enjoy and implement these strategies and watch your business soar!

Peggy McColl
New York Times Best Selling Author

Introduction

I love my business. It's both fun and incredibly fascinating. It's always changing. Being in business doesn't come without its challenges, but that's what makes us grow, right?

There are always new products being introduced and new applications for products. In fact, if I had a nickel for every time someone said, "OMG, that's so cool!" you and I would be in Hawaii. It's a cool business and people love to see their logo on products.

Through years of study of the mind I've come to learn why promotional products work: we're sensory beings. We see, hear, smell, taste and touch. SENSORY MEDIA is the only advertising medium that appeals to all the senses plus it's usually given as a gift. And we love receiving gifts!

Now, understand that I take my fun seriously. Helping companies use SENSORY MEDIA effectively requires a keen understanding about branding and marketing and how SENSORY MEDIA integrates into the bigger picture. The bigger picture always starts with the question, "Why?"

Here is a typical conversation we might have with a new customer.

Customer: Hello. We need some pens for our trade show.

Us: Oh, trade show, eh? (We're Canadian) Sounds interesting! Tell me about the show.

Customer: It's an industry show we do every year and we need pens to give out.

Us:	Why do you want to give out pens?
Customer:	Because we need something to hand out.
Us:	Sounds like a great idea but why do you want to give them out in the first place?
Customer:	Because we need something with our name on it.
Us:	Okay, that's fair. And how much business are you getting from the pens you've given out in the past?
Customer:	Uh, I don't know. (Sidebar: people don't usually think pens are measurable)
Us:	Well, let me ask you this question then. Is the goal of your show to increase visibility and ultimately generate sales?
Customer:	Absolutely!
Us:	If we were to put together a simple strategy that would do just that – increase visibility and generate sales – would that be of interest to you?

If the person calling has any stake whatsoever in that show being a success, the answer to that question is surely a resounding, "YES!"

You see, what I've found in the years of working with people and companies to help them build, communicate and increase the visibility of their brand is that they typically start with the "what": the product.

The truth is that while pens might be the perfect tool for the trade show, we need to first take a step back and take a look at the "Why?"

- Why is the company in business? (their purpose, mission and unique selling proposition)
- Why are they doing the show? (Increase sales? Visibility? Demonstration? Education?)

Once we have the core message nailed down and understand the purpose and goals of the show, then we can move into *what* SENSORY MEDIA communication tools will be used, and *how*.

But there's more, and the principals are universal and can be applied to all brands, in all circumstances.

At any time it's not enough to just have groovy pens or handouts with your name on it. That's just one aspect of branding.

Understand that your brand is happening all the time. Your brand isn't just a logo or a sign or a message on a product. Your brand is a set of expectations and a series of experiences that your customers and potential customers will have with you.

To increase your brand's visibility you need to pay attention to the small stuff. There are so many subliminal clues you're handing out about your brand; many of which you may not even be aware.

Pay attention to consistency. It's important to use the same colours fonts, and messaging in any and all communication. We, humans, like consistency. It says, "stability" to us. Create a style guide and stick to it. Consistently deliver on expectations, as well.

Pay attention to how your tools integrate. There needs to be synergy between online and off line messaging.

The most important aspect is to remember that people are brands (or brand ambassadors). People create experiences. You can have the best T.V. commercial and website but if the interaction between a customer and an employee doesn't go well, the branding chain is broken. The good news is, understanding the power people have to give brands life, gives you enormous potential to increase visibility in multiple ways.

The trade show example is just one of many circumstances where you can increase brand visibility. I hope the 50 ways outlined in the following pages get you started to reaching your BIG goals.

Succeed deliberately!

#1

Create Ambassadors

One rich pool of potential ambassadors is your team. Whether you realize it or not they are the ones who talk about their work and your brand on a daily basis. Give them something to talk about.

Team welcome kits are a great opportunity to put tangible messages into people's hands right off the bat. Usually the "welcome kit" includes corporate information, perhaps info on company benefits and safety plans, but not always do these kits arm the employee with ways in which to share positive messaging about the company.

By giving the team member a shirt, water bottle (or travel cup) and phone charger, you're giving them items that they'll use. Here's what happens:

1) The employee is appreciative of the gesture and the gift instills a good feeling about the company right off the bat (everyone loves gifts)

2) The employee, when using these gifts, is spreading the corporate branding around visually as well as through conversations likely sparked by the use of the product

3) (This one is the biggie) When, in addition to your logo, you include one line about the corporate philosophy, a signature product, social responsibility, or something that you want your staff member to learn and share about the company, you empower an "ambassador" with what messages to share. It doesn't cost any more to add that line to any product but the results of sharing exactly what you want to are huge.

2

Join a
community organization

If your business is local then joining a local club or organization is a great way for members to get to know you. It doesn't matter if the organization you select is a business group or a sports team. If there are like minds with a common goal or purpose, you are in a position to support that purpose while getting to know other members in your community.

You might think that by joining a community basketball league that the only thing you'll accomplish is a great workout and camaraderie. The group of guys or gals you're playing with are likely business professionals themselves. Getting to know them and looking for ways to support them is an ideal integration, exercising your mind, your body and your heart.

3

Speak at a university

There are plenty of extracurricular organizations looking for real-life speakers at any college or university.

The college or university tends to be a community on its own. The students rarely leave the campus and much of what they do and learn revolves around the campus lifestyle.

The clubs and organizations in which students participate thrive on the information shared by practitioners who can bridge the knowledge between the text book and the real world.

Research the clubs and see which most aligns with a topic you're particularly passionate about. The win for the students is getting to hear from you. Your wins include the practice you'll get from sharing your presentation, learning from the questions the students ask and the sharing they'll likely do of your message or brand as a result of your being there. Remember to give them a tangible hand-out to keep your message alive.

If you don't feel like you're a good enough speaker, there are groups and programs that can help you build effective presentations skills. That's easy. Most importantly, remember that if you care enough about the people in the room to want to give them the best you can, your authenticity will be your trump card.

4

Coin a phrase around a hole sponsorship

We're talking about "increasing" visibility so this idea is a way to make what you may already be doing more effective.

Ford sponsors a basketball spot entitled "drive of the game", a featured play that is highlighted with Ford's name. Get it? Drive of the game?

So the next time you're asked to sponsor a hole at a golf tournament, ask to sponsor it as a contest. Some contests we've done are:

"Raise the roof" Yes, a roofing company sponsored the hole and anyone who landed on the green in a single shot received a prize.

"Drain it" This was sponsored by a plumbing company. The longest putt won the prize, a set of taps.

"Everything's coming up roses". A flower shop was behind this contest. The person whose drive came closest to the urn of flowers in the middle of the fairway won a bouquet of flowers.

The trick is to make a contest that is:

1) Relative to your business so that the contest name is memorable

2) Duplicable so that you can implement it at any number of tournaments

3) One that will not slow the game down

Often times you have additional opportunity to be promoted before, during and the tournament with your clever contest. The visibility goes far beyond a sign on the hole.

▼

5
Write a book

I know what you're thinking, "I'm not a professional writer." It doesn't matter. What's important is that you have a message to share and people want your information.

There are ways to self-publish a book with a ghost writer and increase your visibility with your unique message.

Some professionals use their book as a gift during speaking engagements. Others leverage their book through collaborate channels or even on the website. The book being a stand-alone success does take considerable effort, not only to write, but to market, but that, too, is an option.

I'll maintain that it's a "simple" strategy but if your goal is to be a *New York Times* best-selling author, then don't misinterpret "simple" for "easy". Developing a book around a specific topic in which you're competent and bringing in partners to help position you as an expert are powerful.

Decide on a topic then reach out for assistance. You'll be glad you did!

6

Join in for a cause

This is a big category because there is a multitude of ways you can increase your visibility by aligning with a cause. And it doesn't have to be a commitment of millions of dollars to be effective.

Essentially, people prefer to buy from companies who display a commitment to being socially responsible. So choose a charity that you're passionate about or where can see your organization making a difference.

If your customer base is local, choose a local charity. If your audience is national, go national. If your reach is global, and you would like to choose one charity for simplicity and consistency, support a movement that would directly or indirectly resonate with your global customer base..

Your support of the charity could be your time, donating your products, raising funds or awareness, supporting campaigns or even creating a campaign of your own.

Your exposure is enhanced because while you're citing your charitable initiatives on your website, your charity partner is sharing your brand on theirs.

The key is to carve out a giving plan with one main charitable partner. Jump in and let your customers see the amazing work you're doing to lift us all.

7
Help a friend

Expanding your visibility is always about looking for ways to be more. A great way to be more is to give more.

If your friend needs help moving, offer to do what you can and wear your company logoed shirt when you do. You'll be sure to spark conversation with other helpers about what you do.

If your friend is starting a business, be a sounding board. Your ability to listen and mirror back ideas to grow will be extremely appreciated and likely spark new-found respect for what you do.

If your friend is getting in shape for a big climb or bike ride, offer to buddy-up. You'll be healthier for it and the people you'll meet during the challenge will enhance your circle of influence.

The Law of Reciprocity says that what you give away comes back. Give first.

8
Co-brand

Piggy-backing on something that already exists is a great way to leverage current market engagement. Why reinvent the wheel when you can co-brand?

For example, if a car dealership is giving out cleaning cloths to their customers who come in for service, and those customers are also your target audience, offer to split the cost of the cloth to include your brand message. The dealership already has a loyal following. If your brands are complementary then both you and the dealership are adding value to the customer by saying that you support each other's service.

Same holds true for charities, real estate agents, dentists, banks, food producers… you name the business and likely they have a following. Find out what they're giving to their customers and offer to co-brand it.

9

Identify the camera angle

When you watch a hockey game on T.V. the logos you see on the boards cost more than the logos that are on the boards under the cameras. The exposure the logos on the boards that the camera picks up during the game get millions more impressions than those the camera doesn't pick up.

If the camera is photographing golfers at tee-off, a right-handed golfer will sport the logo on the right side of his cap when the camera is behind him (it usually is at tee-off). The left side of the cap will receive less exposure.

It may not sound like a huge deal but when you're talking about logo placement on things that receive multiple sponsorships then you'll want to be mindful. I refer to banners, screens, power points and t-shirts with multiple logos, "Logo soup". No one logo stands out. If you're being stirred in a pot with other sponsors, look for a position that will help you stand out. Think of the concept of the "camera angle" and maximize your visibility.

#10
Create an enthusiastic culture

The culture in any organization will determine what your team members are saying about your company. Know that they are talking about where they work every single day. Multiply those conversations by the number of people and you realize how many people you can have working for you or against you (or both at the same time).

Creating a positive culture first means that everyone needs to be on the same page. "Flat" organizations (where all members work as equals) as opposed to vertical organizations (where there is a clear hierarchy) tend to have better chance at creating a genuine culture. When the President flips burgers at the company picnic and where "intrapreneurialism" is encouraged in an organization, you create more enthusiastic buy-in with members who genuinely care about the company and the brand.

When people have a strong sense of pride belonging to your organization, it's a natural tendency for them to defend and support company philosophies and actions. They'll share positively because they're more engaged and enthusiastic about where they invest their time.

Understand that you will increase visibility with staff one way or another. Creating a thriving, energetic and enthusiastic culture ensures your visibility by multiplying in a positive way.

11

Make standing in line fun

Have you ever stood in line at the bank and watched T.V. while you're waiting for the next teller? Or been entertained by CNN at the airport when your flight was delayed? These are great ways that services take your mind off waiting.

There's another really cool format of video advertising whereby, rather than the screen being a broadcast channel, it's a series of games, puzzles and ads. It's a loop format that refreshes every certain number of minutes (if the line is moving properly you shouldn't see the message twice) and is a series of interesting facts, trivia questions or any numbers of mind puzzles, with advertising messages woven in.

You have a great captive audience – line minders – but remember most people also have their phones out when they're waiting. If your ad has a hash tag or contest or call to action, you have a greater chance of increasing visibility to asking the viewer to take some action on their phone.

#12

Dress human billboards

Now, you could take this in a literal sense and create billboards for people to wear around. They're a bit cumbersome but I imagine they do get attention.

What I'm suggesting, though, is something as simple as a T-shirt. It's a way to expand your reach without anyone having to change their lifestyle i.e. they're going to wear something, why not wear your brand?

People love to be billboards and will pay dearly for it. What we wear is an expression of ourselves. We wear slogans, brands, quotes, graphics and teams that we support. We're natural "brand endorsers". In fact, we're such strong "brand endorsers" that we're willing to pay handsomely to show that we stand for brands like Roots®, Abercrombie®, Raptors®, Starbucks®, Steelers®, Nike®, Pinehurst®, Led Zeppelin®, Budweiser®, the Toronto Maple Leafs®, Adidas®, Justin Bieber, and hundreds of others.

If your brand is not a household name then you may need to be a little more creative about what that "billboard" says to ensure your audience wears your message. Simply putting a logo on the shirt may not be enough. It might require a groovy graphic, reflective properties, fashion-forward colours or styling or a statement that resonates with your market.

Industry surveys reveal that the T-shirt generates, on average, 235 impressions. A $5.00 t-shirt could cost just over two cents per impression. If you're already handing out garments, look at the way in which you distribute them, to whom, and what message is contained on the shirt. It's easy to increase visibility when you've got such a big canvas to worth with.

#13
Wrap up the java

Sometimes it's those really obvious opportunities that get missed... like coffee cup sleeves.

If you need to generate visibility for an upcoming event, you'll want to be in as many faces as you can in a short period of time.

Coffee cup sleeves are perfect for instant visibility and by providing sleeves to an organization that typically uses their own, you're eliminating their cost without requiring any more or different action on their part.

The coffee house may be a great place to submit your sleeves to get your campaign off to a start. If the coffee house is open to ways in which to support community initiatives or local businesses they may welcome the zero-cost investment of using your sleeves for a short period of time.

If you're a for-profit company and it's your own brand of which you want to enhance exposure, offering your sleeves to companies who provide coffee service to corporations might be a great plan. Again, the sleeves are free to the end user, it's no added effort for the distributor, and your message is seen by a whole new set of buyers. If the coffee provider is already giving sleeves, offer to co-brand them.

14
Increase pledges

When charities look for sponsoring donors they sometimes outline only specific donor opportunities to make it a fair playing field for all potential donors One opportunity that is rarely offered is one that will increase pledges. This is a win-win like no other and worth asking to create the spot.

Here's how it works.

You offer to donate a specified gift to every fundraiser who hands in pledges at a stated amount. Let's say the charity's average pledge is $75 but they'd really love to see that average increase to $250. You offer a gift to everyone who increases their pledges to $250. Every time the challenge is shared, you get visibility. Then each of the successful fundraisers receives a gift from you – more visibility.

It's actually a triple win. The charity increases their average pledge, you increase your visibility and the fundraisers receive a gift for their extra effort. Doesn't get any better than that!

#15

Paint the floor

This is definitely my biggest "Aha" this year.

Everyone is walking around staring at their phones. They're looking down. So why are we advertising up?

In the big league, sporting event surfaces have become big-ticket sponsorship spots. The ice, basketball court, tennis court, and the like are logoed. But think, where we looking down on a regular basis? Universities, shopping malls, convention centres, chiropractors' offices, and salons for starters. It wouldn't take much to increase your visibility with a targeted audience using catchy floor graphics in one of these streams.

#16
Say more when you're away

The standard email out-of-office message goes something like this: Thank you for your message. I am out of the office from this time to that time. Here is someone with whom you can connect in my absence.

Can you see the missed opportunity?

Sharing that you're not there is respectful so that people don't expect an immediate response from you.

However, this is an incredible opportunity to share more! What are you working on that you want everyone to know about? What else can you say in this message to increase visibility about a product, a service, an event, a launch, a new study, something keen on your website, your Facebook page or an article you posted on LinkedIn?

If you write your out-of-office message like you're speaking to someone, you'd likely write it a little more conversationally. And if there is something you want people to know about, this is a great place to share that information. It'll be seen even when you're not around.

#17

Decorate bodies

The millennial generation is said to be the most decorated generation in history. Millennials tell their story on their bodies. Each person is a unique work of art both inside and out.

Just like the t-shirt where the wearers endorse the brand, a temporary tattoo is a phenomenal way to share your message. We think of temporary tattoos as interactive show-stoppers just for children, and they're great for kids' camps and initiatives, but think about team building, event entrance, word focus, and game-day spirit.

The cool thing about temporary tattoos is just that; they're temporary. That means you can deliver a variety of messages over time OR use consistent impressions of the same message to make you a household word.

#18
Utilize phone-power

Where would we be without our cell phones!?!

Cell phones have become a necessary tool to us. Not only do we use them to communicate with one another, but we stay connected on a much grander scale. Being able to do bank transfers, order flowers, read a newspaper, capture and share photos and videos, check the game score, turn down the thermostat in the house, and video chat with friends from our phones is our way of life.

What that means to you is that when your brand is displayed on or with an individual's phone, you can potentially generate hundreds of impressions per day. Decorating phone cases, wallets, chargers, cords, home-key buttons, screen cloths or charms with your brand almost guarantees you'll be seen.

#19
Follow the eye

Our eye follows an "F" pattern when we read on the web. In fact in a study by the Nielsen Group this holds true all across articles, e-commerce sites, and search engine results. People almost always browse in an F-shaped pattern.

What this means to you is that if you put your most important copy on the left-hand side, you'll get more of the meat of your message absorbed by your reader.

Simple enough!

20
Look up... look *way* up

In this day and age where everyone is staring down at their cell phones, there are still those who are looking up… with nothing to see but "beige". I'm talking about ceilings.

Now think of a captive audience who is looking up. An athlete doing bench presses at the gym? A dental patient having a cleaning?

Give them a creative message to look at.

21

Leave them wanting more

It's not unusual for a business professional to share 100-200 emails a day.

With that in mind, how are you leveraging what people might be reading in your signature? Are you giving them simply contact information (or worse, nothing) or do you include something trending in your world?

An ideal addition is something that rotates perhaps every month. A message that stays long enough to generate enough impressions to stick, but not too long that it's become a subliminal message and is overlooked.

If you want to track the effectiveness of your message, include a link or call to action. If you want to get the Law of Reciprocity working in your favour, simply offer some advice or a way in which you can help.

It's always about building relationships. This is a great spot to enhance them.

22
Include a QR code

QR codes are easy to create. If you're not familiar with them, they're the patterned squares that when you click with your cell phone, you're linked directly to a page or information. (I heard one case history the other day that a snow plow company imprinted QR codes on ice scrapers and gave them to customers. When the customer clicked on the code, it immediately triggered a call to the snow plow company to request an urgent visit.)

QR codes can be imprinted on just about anything – banners, gum wrappers, pet dishes, t-shirts, rally towels... the list goes on and on. Take visibility to the next level – beyond just a logo – to encourage your customer, or potential customer, to actually engage with you. After all, the more they know about you, the more likely they are to buy from you.

23
All good ideas start on a napkin

Napkins are one of the world's shortest advertising messages but in restaurants and bars, they're super effective. Yes, a drink gets popped onto the one on the table and you wipe your dribbles with the other, however, napkins are perfect for a quick burst of messaging while you're waiting for your order to be delivered.

The "increase" isn't because you put a logo on the napkin; the "increase" is because you were sharp enough to add something catchy or interactive to the imprint.

Tell a joke, invite them to an event, add a QR code, or suggest a 'share' on social media using a hash tag. Increasing visibility is about that second message beyond just a logo.

24
Tack on a vehicle sign

Doing a complete body wrap of your vehicle might not sound so appealing for your personal vehicle, but something removable can have great impact when you need it.

Magnetic door signs, window cling decals, removable bumper stickers or simply a sign in the window can be more than enough to get added attention.

If the first thought is to put your logo on that door sign, think beyond. What do you want people to do or how do you want them to feel, as a result of seeing your sign? You could be creating awareness that your service is now available in their neighbourhood, but in a way that helps them feel drawn to call. Get creative about that message by saying something like, "Another beautiful bouquet of flowers is being delivered." or "When you're ready to get in the best shape of your life, call (trainer)." Create your sign with language that would help people imagine the rewards associated with dealing with you.

25
Take up golf

Remember the last time you said to your friend, "I need to get some IT work done at the office.", or "I'm thinking of selling my house.", or "My lease is almost up on my car, I'd like to look at something new." Your friend's response, likely, was "I gotta guy..." Wouldn't it be great to be that "guy" who everyone wants to refer?

There is a lot of promoting that goes on between golf members. Here's why I think that is.

You can learn a lot about a person by playing golf with them. For four and a half hours you're put through a series of tests: for starters, physically, morally and mentally. Your patience is tested. Your sense of humour is tested. Your ability to focus is tested. Your friendship, conversation skills, tolerance and level of competitive spirit is tested. You have nowhere to hide. Your best and your worst are revealed on the golf course.

When you join a club and play with the same individuals week after week, you really get to know them. It's not like knowing someone from a business meeting. On a golf course, you really get to know them.

And if it's true that we deal with people we like and trust (and I think it is) then you'll gain some great ambassadors by simply enjoying the game of golf.

#26
Give something away

If you're familiar with the Law of Reciprocity then you'll know it is a sub-law of the Law of Vibration. The Law of Reciprocity essentially states that any thought energy sent into the unified field will manifest outcomes in the physical world.

The Law of Reciprocity works between humans, too. You might have recognized in yourself that sometimes you feel like you want to repay someone who has helped you, even though they gave the help without any expectation of receiving something back.

When you can show people – through gifts of legitimate value, without expecting anything in return – that you're a person who understands their needs and wishes to help, you'll naturally attract people who will wish to support you.

The wrong way to use the Law is to give things away with big expectations or attachments. That's not giving, that's trading and people eventually see through it. Giving has to be authentic. Give because you want to help, thank, appreciate, recognize, celebrate, educate or simply make someone's day better. Givers really do gain.

27

Do a survey

Here is why I think surveys are trending: competition. I think it has to do with the fact that Millennials are seen as the least loyal of the generations.

The good and the bad on Millennials is that they have a global reach, a "me first" attitude, are always multi-tasking and are tech-dependent. They're more socially responsible than the previous generation and learn best through interactivity. Any loyalty they may have with a brand will be because the company is planet-friendly (or aligned with another global movement that resonates) and has their individual needs firmly planted in the corporate culture.

If companies are not doing surveys regularly to clearly identify who their customers are and what they're doing to maintain their business, they're likely doing more talking than listening. If you're not serving your customers in a way that works for them, someone else will.

Empowering survey results will come as a result of asking very strategic questions and give you insights into leveraging your brand easily.

28
Keep plenty of white space

Since space costs money, it's not uncommon for advertisers to want to tell as much of their story as possible in a finite amount of space. Using "white space" in your ad employs the "less is more" principle and is very effective.

Decide on the core message you want to deliver. Decide next on the call-to-action you want to happen as a result. Give contact info and let it go.

White space has a retro look to it – by today's standards is trendy – and ensures that you focus on exactly and only the limited information on the page.

I don't think I've ever seen an ad with just a QR code, a question and lots of white space. Sounds risky but I would bet dollars to donuts it would be more effective than a cluttered ad with no clear focus and an overwhelming amount of information.

Albert Einstein said, "Everything should be made as simple as possible, but not simpler." We like simple. When you deliver "simple" you're making it easier for people to understand your business and connect.

▼

#29
Volunteer for a committee position

Whether it's your local Chamber, a charity, a not-for-profit, an association or a business group, taking a committee position is a recipe for expansion.

Your mind expands because you'll be doing work in the new position that is different from that in your business.

Your heart expands because you realize the work you're doing is so meaningful and appreciated by hundreds if not thousands of people.

Your network expands because you're sitting at the table with other business professionals who are outside your industry; people you likely wouldn't have a connection with but with whom you can mutually add value.

Your brand expands by the sheer nature that you, yourself, are visible.

If you want to go the extra mile in helping your market, volunteer for a charity or association that aligns with your business. That gives you a first-hand look at what your audience is experiencing. For example: if your products or services suit an aging population, perhaps sitting on a board or committee that supports seniors is a great way to get behind the scenes and really learn of their challenges. Expand your visibility and your business by giving a little bit of your time.

30

Stack the deck

One of our customers has a big, indoor putting green in their office. Another has a ping pong table. Creating a place for fun activity in the workplace is becoming more common and for good reason. It gets people moving and interacting in ways they wouldn't otherwise through their work.

If you're looking for a way to increase visibility in the modern office, offer up something game related or some playing cards they can put in their lunchroom.

Make your playing cards true to your brand, not only with the colours, but with the look and feel. If your brand is light-hearted, create the face of the cards with cartoon characters or even members of your team. If your brand is more traditional, reflect that in the design of the cards.

Hint: no one will say no to extra cards they can take home.

▼

31
Keep it flowing

Let's talk about both water bottles and bottled water. Both work.

First: bottled water. If you keep bottled water in your office for your staff or customers, or even if you carry it around yourself, allowing some-one else's brand to be the feature on the label is missing an opportunity to share a message. Let's face it. You're paying for the water anyway, so why not create a label with a message that would make your customers and staff feel really special? You can even coin a phrase around feeling refreshed or invigorated because of your association. The label is a full-colour canvas just waiting to make a statement on your behalf. Add a QR code, consecutive numbering or call-to-action and you've got a fabulous donation to a charitable event.

Second: water bottles. They are the perfect vehicle in which to distribute your literature. We need to be thinking of reducing our packaging and by sharing our "message in a bottle" – and ON the bottle – we're doubling up on exposure. Gone are the days when we simply put a logo on something. That's merchandising. We're marketing. What would you like to say on that water bottle that will help your customer understand you're there to serve them?

Pop a second gift – a t-shirt, golf tees, sunscreen, a ticket to an event (better yet, make the water bottle the ticket to the event!!) – and your message is delivered in an environmentally-sound package.

32

Create a memorable experience

There is no form of advertising more powerful than word-of-mouth. By today's standards, you don't hold your brand, your customers do. Your customers are going to talk and share amongst themselves about how they experience you. This has always been the case, however in the years B.I. (before internet), if you did something well, your customer would tell someone. If you did something poorly your customer would tell 10 people. That was pretty much the rule of thumb.

Now that we're in the age of internet, there is no telling just one person. Thousands, if not millions, can experience your brand and will feed back to you, and the rest of the world, how they feel about it.

It's not just about your product or service. It's about the entire experience and the experience includes people. My son, 22, and I were in an exclusive designer store looking at some travel bags. A security person asked if we needed help. We replied that we were fine checking things out on our own. The security person said we weren't allowed to look at the bags on the (open) shelf without a sales person and summoned someone to help us. The second person again, asked if we needed help. Again, we said that we were fine. The sales person felt compelled to share with us that the bags had security tags on them and could not be removed from the shelf (we already noticed that and hadn't planned to remove them). The "ambassadors" were rather unwelcoming and the experience was belittling. It was enough to turn us off the brand.

Conversely, years ago, I walked into the Lexus dealership. I was in track pants and my son accompanied me. He was only about 12 at the time. On the outside we probably didn't "appear" like Lexus customers. A sharply-dressed, very polite sales person approached us and we began to discuss my current vehicle and what next vehicle might better suit my needs. The conversation was respectful and intelligent and he proceeded to take us for a test drive, explaining how my potential new car compared to what I had. I was clear with him that I still had a year on my current lease and wasn't ready to buy, but there were no road blocks in his effort to ensure I had everything I needed for when I was ready to make my decision. The time came. I returned to that dealership and asked for that sales person. Fast forward 10 years to date, I just ordered my fourth Lexus from the same sales person. The dealership's consistent, quality service has me tweeting about them and now including them in this book.

Be mindful of the experience you're creating for your customers during every encounter. Ensure front-line staff is enthusiastic and knowledgeable about your brand and that their focus is on creating a warm and inviting customer experience each and every time.

33

Sponsor a speaker

Picture this. The audience of 650 members is so quiet you can hear a pin drop. They're anxiously anticipating the arrival of the keynote speaker. You get to introduce the speaker and before you do, you share a story and a message about your brand to this captive audience.

Sponsoring a speaker is an ideal way to have a few, very quality minutes with an audience ready to listen. Often that few minutes is where many sponsors stop and they limit their visibility potential.

Organizers typically welcome gifts that you wish to put on the tables, a draw you'd like to hold, and an insert into the program outline. You can enhance your visibility by exercising all touch points with this audience beyond your few minutes on the podium. Tie everything together – your program insert, your gift, your draw and your presentation – and you've got a memorable combination.

34
Change the media you're using

When people start businesses, the first thing they typically do is get a website. A good web designer will ask you why you think you need a website to ensure if you're going to invest the money, that it's the right tool and works in a way that supports your growth. Depending on your market and budget, a designer may even question whether or not a website is necessary.

It's not necessary to set up common channels just because everyone else does it. What's important is that you look carefully at how each medium works, whose attention it's directed towards, and if it would ultimately create the visibility and value you're looking for.

We designed a direct mail campaign for a golf course. The campaign was for the banquets department to encourage local businesses to host their company Christmas party and seasonal meetings at the club. We identified 200 businesses in the area who would be excellent candidates. We phoned each business to get the person whose job it was to book those events. Then we created a mailer, addressed by hand and stamped, to go to each of the individuals. Having names and numbers logged, it was easy to follow up to answer their questions and book their rooms. The mailing was a big success. What's more is that the golf club had a new following of customers and even more importantly, a list that was golden.

The next year the golf club decided to return to advertising in the newspaper, because it was easy. It certainly wasn't less expensive but it was less effort.

You need to look at the scope of what your medium can deliver to you and assess if it's bringing the exposure and results. It sounds great to be on all the social media channels but it can be time-consuming and an expense - as opposed to an investment - if your customers aren't engaging on those channels. Target the medium that maxes out your visibility with your customers.

35
Sponsor a book

If writing a book isn't in the cards, try sponsoring one.

It's not a tactic used often but can increase visibility in markets you previously had only a hope of getting in front of. Every time someone reads the book they'll see your message.

Research authors who write or speak about your industry, your charity, culture, operating system, country, or who educate groups or individuals who are of interest.

Offer to sponsor their next publication with a page that shares your brand message. Keep it simple and code the page so you can track the queries when they arrive.

▼

36

Would you like fries with that?

Business is about solving a problem or helping someone improve their life as a result of what you do.

When you think of it that way – that you're a solutions provider – then asking if they'd like to sample a second service is a way to help them beyond the obvious. It's also a great way to increase visibility of a product or service of which your customers may not be aware.

During a one-month period we asked every customer with whom we spoke on the phone if they used sticky notes and shared that we had the most popular size Post-it note ® pad on special. A few things happened:

1) We initiated conversations about the effectiveness of those little stickies (at the time, the statistics said that on average 2.5 people see the message on each note).

2) Additional conversations about creative application and copy emerged

3) We were seen as solutions-providers by helping people purchase the right adhesive note for their needs

4) Our sales of Post-it notes ® were unprecedented that month.

By asking one question, we increased visibility of a product that everyone used but not everyone knew we carried.

Decide what product or service you'd like to highlight and have your front line people ask just one question.

37

Cross promote

There is likely another service provider who deals with the exact customer you're looking to capture. Since it would be expensive to create a marketing program all your own, it makes more (dollars and) sense to tap into someone who already has an established relationship with the target client.

The question you need to ask is, "Which service comes before or after mine?"

For example, if you're a dry cleaner, then a potentially collaborative service is one that sells the very items you clean. Where are the dress shops, men's wear boutiques, and duvet and blanket stores? Drop off a stack of promotional items for those retailers to hand out a point-of-purchase. The promotional item would be imprinted with your contact info, an offer and a code. The code allows you to track which retailer generated the business. Your agreement with the retailer could be that they receive a percentage of each cleaning sale OR you could have a reciprocal arrangement whereby the retailers could advertise their specials in your dry cleaning store with their own gifts and coupons.

You're adding value to the dress shop and men's wear boutiques by them offering a gift and coupon to their customers. By the retailer sharing the gift it is implied endorsement, which is added encouragement for the customer to do their dry cleaning with you.

This collaborative process is an ideal leveraging tool for both B2B and B2C models.

#38

Give canvassers a gift

At any given time there are likely dozens of charities, not-for-profits or associations asking for your sponsorship or participation. There are a number of ways in which you can contribute but since we're talking about increasing visibility for your brand, try this one on for size.

Many charities have canvassing components. Whether it's simply a door-to-door or friends-and-neighbours campaign or something event-driven like a walk or run, individuals are asked to solicit donations during a certain time frame to support the cause or an initiative.

Offering a financial donation is always well-received but perhaps, instead, you could offer a product or service gift for each of the canvassers or event attendees. Volunteers work hard to generate much-needed dollars but at the end of the day have nothing to show for it. We both know that's not why they do it, but why not reward them with a small gift of thanks?

If the gift is something relevant and is one of your products, then you just created a warm feeling of appreciation, all the while sharing your brand with people you would otherwise not have in your pipeline.

39
Share something valuable

In October of 2013 I started writing, "Aha Moment Mondays". They are short insights that are delivered to our customers, colleagues and friends every Monday morning. AMM was designed as a way to highlight aspects of our lives as professionals, with a business focus and spiritual undertone. Sometimes we ask people questions or suggest action as a result of the message, but we never sell in it.

The Aha's are usually under a 60-second read (in fact, we give you the anticipated reading time at the start) and is a way in which we can share insights and information and inspire everyone to have an exceptional week. The open rate is high and people tell us the Aha's give them something interesting to think about and inspire a positive outlook.

Whether you decide to write a newsletter, simply share an article or formulate your insights on a blog, share something valuable. Here's the key: write with empathy.

There is a multitude of information out there and quite frankly most of us are on overload. But when you share something you know will positively impact your customer, and that it is clear your focus is clearly on helping them have more fun and work more easily, people will look forward with anticipation to what you have to say.

▼

#40
Enter your team into a charity walk

This is a phenomenal team-building exercise with so many wins in visibility.

When you enter you and your colleagues into a charity walk, two things happen: strategizing and bonding.

Team members will typically decide on a fundraising goal then brainstorm on how, individually and collectively, they can achieve it. In the process, the common denominator of the walk brings people together in a setting in which they wouldn't otherwise participate. Of course the charity receives much-needed funds, and your team, donned in their team T's, shoe laces, head bands and rally towels, make for an incredible front-page splash on your website.

Buyers like to work with companies who exhibit clear social responsibility and your website – both internet and intranet – is the perfect ground to profile members and encourage those social media shares.

The added bonus is how many times your team members will wear their team shirts after the walk. The conversations about the company's values and the brand will carry on long after you cross the finish line.

41
Give the task to students

Where does your company hold creative brain-storming sessions? Around a board room table? That's typically the answer. We don't often give it that much thought. When we rally our team we typically use the company board room or rent a hotel space with, yes, another board room. If it's a common place for everyone, it's not much of a nurturing environment for creativity. You need to shake things up a bit.

But why not get some new brains in the storming session by handing over the challenge to students?

Designing a contest for students studying marketing, engineering, entre-preneurialism, or whatever faculty aligns with your problem, you're not only going to receive brand-new ideas, you're getting brand new cheerleaders.

Students love an outside, real-life case history to work on. It brings their studies full circle. It gives them a chance to interact with a potential future employer and have a positive impact on a real problem.

You'll enjoy some exceptional creativity and the students will be your new voice.

42

Create a focus group

Typically the stated purpose of assembling a focus group is to acquire feedback. However, done well, the focus group can also be the perfect breading ground to grow your brand.

It's tough to think like your audience when you, yourself, don't represent the demographic. For that reason, creating a focus group to try out a new product or see if your ad campaign or website is going to fly is a great investment.

Acquiring quality feedback is job-one; however, if the experience for the attendees is a positive one, you offer them a special gift (over and above any other agreed compensation), and you empower them to share something behind-the-scenes about the brand, they'll sing like canaries.

People love to be asked for their advice. Go ahead… ask! It'll be worth it.

43

Be consistent

When you're crystal clear about your brand objectives, then decisions around where and how you're sharing your brand become easy.

What you want to be is consistent with your messaging. In other words your logo, captions, values, font, writing style, colours, and brand images should all integrate into one message that tells a specific story and relates to the audience. Deviating from your colours, fonts or writing style do nothing but create confusion.

Set up an identity guide for your brand and be consistent.

▼

44

Use chair covers

Have you ever walked into a ballroom and seen 100 VIP seats with pieces of paper to indicate whose privilege it is to sit in those seats?

Sponsoring business lectures, forums and conventions can be costly and if the only reward is your logo on a banner, you're not maximizing your investment.

Instead, invest in custom slip covers for the convention floor seats.

All the other sponsors' logos will be flashed on a screen at the opening of the conference and your logo will be there the entire time on the backs of 100 seats.

Custom chair-back covers are inexpensive and an ideal way to maximize your visibility for days at a time.

45
Don't over-connect

Okay, so this one isn't a "do" it's a "don't do".

One really great thing about social media is that it's magnificently easy to connect thousands of people around the globe. But you don't need to connect with everyone for the sake of connecting.

There are social networking junkies who just connect for the satisfaction of watching the numbers go up. Granted, by doing this, they're increasing visibility, but people see through the action of why they're connecting.

In this world of transparency, being authentic about your reasons to connect will generate the kind of visibility you're looking for.

#46
Run a contest

Building traffic and generating results at a trade show take thought and planning. Ideally you'll want to invite participants to attend giving them reason to stop by your booth. Then you'll want to have some activity at your booth to engage the passers-by and learn something about them. Finally, implementing a follow-up mechanism to ensure you make solid contact afterwards is the perfect way to land the sale.

That's trade show success in a nutshell.

But if you want a simple way to beef up visibility at the show, run a contest. Not just a contest where people put their cards or ballots in a box then at the end of the day you draw for a prize; a contest where the attendees need to take a photo, spin a wheel, or do some activity worth entering them into a contest.

Here's the enhanced visibility part. Draw for a contest winner every hour and request to the show organizers that your prize is announced over the PA system each time. Write the script for the announcer to ensure your brand message is clear. That hourly prize announcement (mini-commercial) is assurance that your brand is being shared beyond those who stop by; as well, you'll keep attendees around your floor longer when they know to listen for their name.

47
Know that less is more

In many circles "change" is a four-letter word. We think that people resist change but the truth is people resist being changed. If change doesn't affect them then they're likely indifferent, but if something new means they need to do something new, you might be inviting resistance.

Like an artist releasing too many albums at one time, always pushing something new into the hands of your audience can dilute your brand. While you might think you're innovating by constantly shaking things up with new products and services, your customer may be feeling a little off-balance or overwhelmed, unable to keep up. In fact having too many products in the market place can create a negative effect.

You're more powerful allowing traction for fewer products. Creating visibility is easier when your message is simple and consistent.

▼

48

Remember, it's always about the "why"

Any marketing program needs to have a stated purpose. How else would you measure it, right? More importantly, your corporate mission needs be carried through any and all efforts. Your goal is always to ensure your business is positively impacting lives; that people in your organization are growing as a result of their work, and your community is in better hands because of you.

When you're clear on why you're doing anything, the decisions around all actions become obvious.

In my practice we always ask the question, "Why?" when people are deciding on their SENSORY MEDIA to support their campaign. Often times the answer is, "We just need to give something away."

No you don't; but, if you want to give something away, then you need to know why you're doing it. Only then can you develop a product that fits your client, carries your message and generates impact.

#49
Make it personal

Have you noticed that real estate agents love to give out calendars? They're great advertising pieces because they keep your brand message in front of your customers 365 days a year.

Now here's the issue. If all the real estate agents in the neighbourhood are sending out calendars, which one(s) do you keep? Personally I received 12 this January and I only kept one. Why? Because not only did it have the agent's contact info, it also had my name on it.

The gifts that people keep first and the longest are ones with their name on it. If the gift has the recipient's name on it, it's guaranteed to generate way more impressions than if it had the giver's brand alone. And with today's variable print options, it's easy to create calendars, screen cloths, towels, pens, water bottles, garments and a multitude of other gifts with individual names.

Make it personal.

50
Show up

There is a tremendous amount of work we can get done efficiently by using technology. We can reach thousands of people with the stroke of a key. But we should never lose sight of two facts when it comes to leaving the office.

1) Every decision is made by one person. While you may be connecting with thousands at a time from behind your screen, you can't replace the connection of one-to-one when you're physically in the room

2) You are the gift you bring to the room. Your presence is electric and can't be felt through email or any social media channel. Your in-person energy is incomparable.

Showing up is even more than that, though.

It's not enough to only be physically present if your mind is somewhere else. It's also your emotional attention that counts. It's being focused on who you're speaking to and what you're communicating about at that exact moment. It's being present in mind, body and spirit.

Since we're spiritual beings living in the physical body, know that people you're communicating with will feel it when you're 100% present.

Be all in.

A few closing comments from the author

Thank you for investing your time here today! I hope you enjoyed reading "50 Simply Ways to Increase Brand Visibility" as much as I enjoyed writing them for you.

Actually, it was tough to narrow it down to only 50 ways as there are thousands of strategies we can implement using tangible, SENSORY MEDIA to generate brand impact. In fact, I outline why SENSORY MEDIA is so effective in my first book; *SENSORY MEDIA: Discover the Way to Anchor Your Brand and Be Memorable*. Hop on www.sensorymedia.ca to receive your copy.

And, let's stay connected! I'm anxious to hear your feedback and ideas! Please send any comments and questions to 50SimpleWays@jaeassociates.com. We promise to reply back; as well, will invite you to become a member of our community. And when I say "member", I don't mean just a member of our social media community (though we welcome you there, for sure!). We're organizing a separate membership for those who want insider info on what works, and help to make it happen.

As always,

Succeed deliberately!

Jae M. Rang, MAS
Strategist, Speaker, Author, Mom

About the author

Jae M. Rang, MAS is the Founder and Chief Inspiring Officer of the promotional marketing firm, JAE associates Ltd. Jae's first book: **SENSORY MEDIA, *Discover the Way to Anchor Your Brand and Be Memorable***, hit the Amazon best-seller list the day it launched. In **50 *Simple Ways to Increase Brand Visibility***, Jae opens your mind to generate more buzz with strategies you may already be using, and introduces you to some innovative, new ones.

Jae has won a multitude of image awards for creative campaigns, is the Past Chair of the Promotional Products Professionals of Canada (PPPC), Chair of the PPPC Scholarship Program, 2011 PPPC Hall of Fame inductee, 2014 recipient of the PPPC Humanitarian Award, a Strategist, Speaker Author and, most importantly, Mom.

Jae is people-focused, results-oriented and community-spirited.

Succeed deliberately!

www.ingramcontent.com/pod-product-compliance
Lightning Source LLC
Chambersburg PA
CBHW060619210326
41520CB00010B/1396